FRENCH
FOOD AND DRINK

Françoise Lafargue

Bookwright Press
New York · 1987

FOOD AND DRINK

Chinese Food and Drink
French Food and Drink
Indian Food and Drink
Italian Food and Drink

First published in the
United States in 1987 by
The Bookwright Press
387 Park Avenue South
New York, NY 10016

First published in 1987 by
Wayland (Publishers) Ltd
61 Western Road, Hove,
East Sussex BN3 1JD, England

ISBN 0-531–18130–8
Library of Congress Catalog Card Number:
86–73115

Typeset by DP Press Ltd, Sevenoaks, Kent
Printed in Italy by G. Canale & C.S.p.A., Turin

Cover *A café in the Champs Élysées, Paris.*
Throughout France cafés are popular meeting
places.

Contents

The country of France

With an area of 550,000 square km (211,000 sq mi), France is the largest country in western Europe. It has a population of 55 million, 10 million living in or around Paris, the capital. The country is a republic, which means that it has an elected president. France is divided up into ninety-six administrative *départements* (departments): ninety (including the island of Corsica in the Mediterranean Sea) are situated on the French mainland, and five are *départements d'Outre-Mer* (overseas departments). These overseas departments are Martinique, Guadeloupe, French Guiana, Saint-Pierre-and-Miquelon and Réunion. Martinique and Guadeloupe are islands in the West Indies, north of South America. French Guiana, a former penal colony, is on the northeast coast of South America and is today an

Besides French overseas departments there are also overseas territories. These boys, holding French bread, are from New Caledonia, an overseas territory where the French influence can still be seen.

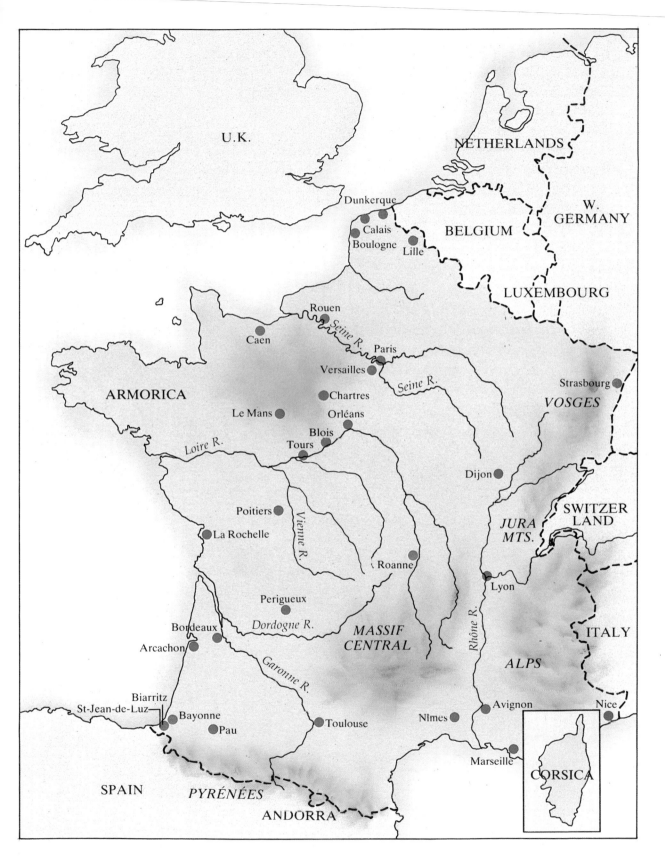

important base from which the European rocket Ariane is launched. The islands of Saint-Pierre-and-Miquelon are off the coast of Newfoundland in Canada, and Réunion is a volcanic island in the Indian Ocean.

France is often referred to as a land of contrast. Although France generally has a temperate climate, neither too cold nor too hot, the climate varies from one region to another. The north, for example, has a lot of rain, whereas the south is dry and much hotter. The landscape, too, varies a great deal. There are three mountain ranges: the Alps in the southeast, the Jura mountains in the east and the Pyrenees which border Spain. There are also three main upland areas, the Massif Central with its extinct volcanoes in central France, the Vosges in the east and the Armorica in Brittany.

There are areas of forest, such as those in the Jura and Vosges mountains, and huge fertile plains, as in the Paris basin and Aquitaine. There are also vast areas of marshland, as in the Carmargue where you can see flamingoes and wild horses, and pine forests like those in the Landes, south and west of Bordeaux.

France, a member of the EEC (the European Economic Community) grows and exports grain, fruit and vegetables. Other major exports are dairy produce and wine. Industry has expanded in France a great deal since World War II but at present it is going through a difficult period, especially in the iron, steel and coal industries.

The tourist industry in France, however, is of growing importance. Every year, hundreds of thousands of people visit France. Many are attracted to Paris with its famous monuments, cathedrals, stores and museums as well as to the nearby seventeenth-century palace of Versailles, built for Louis XIV, and the châteaux of the Loire Valley. The long and varied coastline with fashionable resorts and the mountains with famous skiing centers also attract the tourists. But visitors also come to France to sample some of the best cooking, and the best wines, in the world.

The cathedral of Notre Dame is just one of the many tourist attractions in Paris.

French food in history

Some of the first inhabitants of France were the Gauls, a people of Celtic origin. Their diet consisted mainly of bread and cereals, although they also ate a lot of pork. The Gauls were also fond of geese. These they crammed with wheat flour, a practice that still exists in France today to produce the famous *foie gras* (see page 28) which is exported all over the world.

The Romans invaded in 51 B.C. and occupied France, or Gaul as it was known then. In addition to building roads, bridges, aqueducts and amphitheaters, they also introduced vines and olives to France. Later, soldiers fighting in the Crusades in the Holy Land brought back Mediterranean foods such as dates, rice and spices.

In the sixteenth century, Catherine de Medicis came to France. She was an Italian from Florence and became the wife of King Henry II. She brought her Italian cooks with her and soon the fashion among the aristocracy was to employ cooks from Florence. With these Italian chefs came such foods as artichokes, ice cream, pastry, beans, melons and pasta.

This interest in food and talented chefs continued into the seventeenth century. Condé, a French general, had a chef named Vatel who was preparing a dinner to which King Louis XIV was invited. However, the fish for the main course did not arrive in time and Vatel, feeling dishonored, committed suicide: cooking was taken very seriously. Louis XIV himself held huge banquets for his court, and employed 300 cooks working in the kitchens of his palace at Versailles.

As far back as the time of the Gauls people were raising geese for their livers, a practice that continues in many parts of France today.

The palace of Versailles was built for Louis XIV in the seventeenth century. He employed 300 cooks to work in the kitchens of the palace.

While the aristocracy was enjoying banquets and rich food, the main foodstuffs for the poorer people were bread, cereals, cabbage and beans. Sometimes they would eat pork, but some, too poor to feed pigs, made do with geese, which would get fatter faster and were cheaper to feed. Those who lived near the coast were more fortunate because of the ready supply of fresh fish. However, in 1695 the governor of Dauphiné observed that "the great majority of the inhabitants of this province lived during the winter only from acorns and roots, and now they can be seen eating the grass of the fields and the bark of the trees."

The French Revolution, which started with the storming of the Bastille in 1789, resulted in the excecution of King Louis XVI and his wife, Marie Antoinette. After the French Revolution many of the chefs who had worked for the now exiled nobility opened restaurants in Paris. But these restaurants only served the rich. The poor people of France were often hungry still.

Slowly, things improved for the poorer people. Better farming techniques meant that there was more, and better, food available. With the coming of railroads this food could be distributed throughout France. Today most French people eat well and are able to enjoy their unique cuisine.

These days, French cooking is known internationally for its excellence and richness. Several different cuisines exist, and the French reputation for excellence has been introduced abroad by great French chefs who prepare the classical French cuisine in hotels and restaurants all over the world.

While the peasants were starving, Marie Antoinette, wife of Louis XVI, had this cottage, along with farm buildings, built for her amusement in the grounds of Versailles. She was later executed in 1793.

Producing the food

With three-fifths of the land suitable for cultivation, France is one of the world's leading agricultural nations. France is often called the "granary" of the EEC, and large areas of land are given over to growing cereals, mainly in the Paris and Aquitaine basins where the soils are good and the climate suitable for crop growing. In the Rhône delta region, known as the Camargue, rice is grown, and sugar beet is grown extensively in the north. Potatoes are an important crop in many regions.

Much land is given over to dairy farming, especially in Brittany and Normandy where cows grazing in the lush and green meadows are renowned for their creamy milk. France exports a lot of butter and cheese. Pigs and sheep are also raised and, in recent years, poultry farming has increased.

Warm southern France is now an area of market gardening. The

Normandy is particularly well known for its dairy produce. In this picture you can see Normandy butter being churned.

An orchard in Provence. The growing of fruit is important in warm, southern France.

melons of Cavaillon in the Vaucluse department, and the strawberries, peaches, apricots and tomatoes in the Rhône and Garonne valleys, the olive groves of the Midi and the oranges and clementines of Corsica are particularly famous.

Another important industry is the growing of grapes to make wine. The best wines are produced in the Bordeaux region, and in Champagne and Burgundy.

All along the French coastline, fishing is an important activity. Boulogne is the most important fishing port, and every day trains and trucks leave the port to transport the fish to all parts of the country.

Other ports may specialize in a certain type of fish. Douarnenez, for example, is the major port for sardines and mackerel, Marennes and Arcachon for mussels and oysters, and Saint-Jean-de-Luz is the major port for tuna fish.

Boulogne is France's most important fishing port.

Selling the food

The French spend well over twenty percent of their income on food compared with under ten percent on clothing. These figures reflect the interest the French people have in what they eat. They are always particular about the food they buy and are careful about comparing quality and prices.

In every town there are the small specialist stores like the *boulangerie* (bakery) where bread is baked on the premises at least twice a day, and the *charcuterie* where cold meats, ready-prepared dishes and various types of sausages are sold. However, in recent years these smaller stores have had to fight the growing importance of the big supermarkets and "hypermarkets" which are now to be found all over the country. These huge stores sell everything from clothes and televisions to food and drink. Everything is much cheaper than in the smaller shops, but always of high quality. The hypermarkets are often open until 10 pm six days a week, and visits to these stores often involve the whole family.

In Paris many stores specialize in selling expensive luxury products. At Christmas time, people stand in long lines on the sidewalk, waiting patiently to buy smoked salmon, caviar, *foie gras*, teas and jams at Fauchon or Hédiard (both very famous stores) and delicious chocolates, and cakes from the famous pastry shop, Lenôtre.

Markets are very important to the French. Once or twice a week in each town, in the streets, in a special square or building, a market is held. Sellers and farmers from the surrounding countryside come to town with fruit, vegetables, dairy products, fish and meat to sell.

In 1969 the enormous market at Rungis, 8 km (5 mi) south of Paris, was created to replace the Halles in

Bread is baked at least twice a day in the boulangeries. *This baker still uses a wood-fired oven for his baking.*

the center of the capital. Producers and retailers meet there to sell and buy food which is then taken by big trucks to all parts of France and countries of the EEC.

Fish markets, which are to be found in the sea ports, are also extremely picturesque with their displays of sardines, tuna fish, mussels and oysters. The fishing boats arrive, full of fresh fish which are then unloaded onto the wharf and placed on ice in baskets. They are sold immediately at auction to restaurant-owners, fish markets and housewives.

Lenôtre in Paris is very famous for its chocolates and cakes.

Most towns have a market square. This colorful market is in St. Flour in the department of Cantal.

The meals

Breakfast (*petit déjeuner*)

The French usually start work between 8 and 9 am, so breakfast is early. The meal consists of bread and butter, *croissants* (crescent-shaped rolls), jam or honey. Adults generally drink *café au lait* (coffee with hot milk) and the children will have a bowl of coffee with milk or hot chocolate. More and more people these days might also have fruit juice, cereal or yoghurt. Those who leave home without breakfast often go to a café for *un petit noir* (a small cup of very strong black coffee).

Lunch (*déjeuner*)

Déjeuner is usually between noon and 2 pm. In the provinces stores and offices close down and people go home for lunch. But in Paris, and

The traditional French breakfast is croissants *and* café au lait.

In the big towns many people visit a snack bar for their lunch.

in the big towns, people with only an hour to eat do not have time to go home. These people often stand in line at self-service restaurants, often for the traditional *steak-frites*, a slice of beef with French fried potatoes. Others might just have a sandwich and a drink. Children will either go home for lunch or will eat in the school cafeteria.

At 4 pm, children ask for their *quatre-heures*. This usually consists of bread with jam or chocolate.

Dinner (*dîner*)

Dinner and lunch are more or less alike, whether eaten at home or in a restaurant. The meal will consist of *hors d'oeuvre* or soup, or both (although soup is more usual at dinner), meat or fish with vegetables, followed by salad,

13

cheese and then a dessert (pastry, ice cream or fruit). Bread is usually served with the meal and there is nearly always wine for the adults and mineral water for the children.

Soups are very popular and each region has its specialty. In Auvergne and Alsace there is the *potée* with vegetables, sausages and pickled pork. Cabbage soup is made in central France. In Provence, soups are made with local products such as garlic, sage, thyme, basil, onions, olive oil, sorrel, tomatoes, fish and mussels. The most famous soup of this region is *pistou*, made with garlic and basil. *Pot-au-feu*, a specialty from Burgundy and Lyons, is a typical French dish composed of *bouillon*, boiled beef and vegetables.

To sharpen the appetite for dinner, the custom is to have an *apéritif* with *amuse-gueules* (small cocktail snacks or olives). Coffee is served at the end of the meal, and perhaps a liqueur "*digestif.*"

Supper (*souper*)

After a night out, the tradition in Paris and in the big towns for some people is to have a *gratinée à l'oignon*, an onion soup with bread and cheese.

Soupe à l'oignon *is traditionally served last thing at night, especially in Paris and other big towns.*

Soupe à l'oignon (onion soup)

You will need:
3 large onions, peeled and chopped
1 tablespoon butter
1 tablespoon oil
1 tablespoon flour
3 generous cups cold water
6 slices stale French bread
½ teaspoon salt
pepper
6 tablespoons grated Gruyère or Swiss cheese.

What to do:
Put the butter and oil in a saucepan. When hot, add the onions and flour. (1) Cook for 10 minutes stirring with a wooden spoon until brown. Add the cold water, salt and pepper, mix and boil for another 10 minutes. Heat the oven. (2) In an ovenproof soup tureen, place 3 slices of bread and 2 tablespoons of grated cheese then the other 3 slices of bread and 4 tablespoons of grated cheese. (3) Strain the soup through a sieve and pour it onto the bread and cheese in the tureen. Cook in a hot (400°) oven for fifteen minutes.

Out for dinner

French people like discovering new restaurants. In addition to the expensive *grands restaurants*, run by great chefs, there are several other types of eating places.

The typical French bistro (there are 10,000 in Paris alone!) serves quick meals such as omelette, ham or steak and French fries as well as wine and other drinks. A *petit restaurant* will offer simple home cooking. There are also pizzerias where Italian pizzas and all kinds of pasta are served, and *crêperies*, specialized small restaurants where you can make a complete meal of *crêpes* (pancakes).

Café life

Cafés first appeared in the second half of the seventeenth century and their number increased rapidly. They were places where new ideas were expressed and debates organized.

The oldest café is the Café Procope in the rue de l'Ancienne Comédie in Paris. The café was founded in 1689 and was a favorite meeting-place of many famous eighteenth-century writers. Café Procope is worth visiting, with its paintings, mirrors, special atmosphere and sense of history.

France is a nation of coffee and

In fine weather, most cafés have tables outside, which attract tourists and locals alike.

wine drinkers and on fine days, tables are put outside the cafés and the customers may order a cool drink, a *Pêche Melba* or a *Mystère Médicis* (named after the soprano Nellie Melba and Queen Catherine de Medicis). Today the cafés are nice places for chatting, meeting friends over a drink, playing cards or watching television.

Mystère Médicis

You will need:
vanilla ice cream
ground almonds
2 tablespoons cocoa powder
1 cup milk
vanilla wafers

What to do:
(1) Mix the cocoa and milk, place on the heat and bring to a boil. Take the ice cream from the freezer. Put servings of ice cream into bowls. (2) Sprinkle the ice cream with almonds. (3) Pour the boiling chocolate onto the ice cream. (4) Serve immediately with vanilla wafers.

Safety note: Be very careful when pouring the hot chocolate.

1

3

2

4

National specialties

Most of the dishes that are today considered to be typically French were once the specialty of a particular region until their popularity spread over the whole of France. Some typically French dishes are *steak-frites* (grilled beef with French fries), *pot-au-feu* (braised beef with vegetables), *blanquette de veau* (slices of veal in a cream sauce) and *boeuf bourguignon* (a rich beef stew cooked in wine with onions and carrots). But France is perhaps best known for its bread, cheese and wine.

Above *The French eat a lot of bread. This picture shows a baby enjoying a* pain de campagne.

There is a wide choice of bread available in France, as can be seen from this picture of a boulangerie.

Bread

The French eat a lot of bread, and they have a choice of over seventy different types of bread made from various cereals (corn, rye, barley or buckwheat), and nineteen different shapes. The *baguette*, for example, is long and thin, the *boule* is short and fatter.

Many bakers' shops (*boulangerie*) make their bread traditionally, mixing the dough by hand and baking it in wood-fire ovens. Most people buy their bread fresh every day from their local baker.

However, although there are 1,700 bakeries in the capital, the family-run bakeries are becoming fewer and fewer since today the supermarkets sell all kinds of bread from industrial bakeries which are less expensive.

In the country, the local baker drives from village to village delivering bread. In Paris, the famous baker Poilâne sells bread to many parts of the world, and foreigners have even gone to Paris to learn Poilâne's baking methods.

Pain perdu

You will need:
3 slices stale white French bread
1 cup milk
2 eggs
2 tablespoons sugar
1 pinch salt
a little butter

What to do:
(1) Whisk the eggs, 1 tablespoon of sugar, salt and milk together. Place the slices of bread in a shallow dish. (2) Pour the liquid onto the slices and turn them. Melt the butter in a frying pan and then reduce the heat. (3) Cook the slices in the butter until golden brown on both sides. (4) Sprinkle with the remaining sugar and eat hot.

1

3

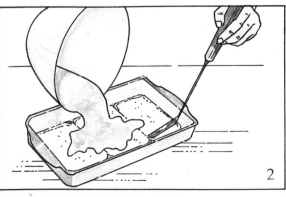
2

4

Butter and cheese

France produces a lot of butter, milk and cheese. The butter from Charente in the Poitou region is particularly famous as is the cream of Normandy. France has the largest variety of cheese in the world with, some people claim, up to 1,000 different kinds.

The French like cheese very much, and several types are always served at meals, before the dessert.

In parts of France cows' milk is used to make soft cheese such as *Brie* and *Coulommiers* from Île-de-France. In central France, in Charente and Touraine for example, semi-soft cheese is made from goats' milk.

The *Cantal* cheese made in Auvergne and the *Comté* from Savoie are both made in the shape of huge wheels, which can weigh up to 80 kg (176 lb) each. The *Comté* is often used in *fondue*, a melted cheese dish.

Alsace, in the east, also produces its own cheese called *Muenster*, which is light-brown in color and strong-smelling. But perhaps most famous of all French cheeses are *Camembert* and *Roquefort*. *Camembert* is a soft cheese made in Normandy. It is always sold in a round box. One can find many imitations in other regions of France. *Roquefort* is a blue-veined cheese made from

France has the largest range of cheeses in the world.

Comté *cheese is made in the shape of huge wheels, some of which can weigh up to 80 kg (178 lb).*

ewes' milk. It is fermented and ripened in caves in limestone cliffs to the south of the Massif Central.

Canapés au Roquefort

You will need:
24 small slices rye bread or toast
7 ounces Roquefort cheese
12 ounces cream cheese
2 tablespoons cream
2 tablespoons ground almonds
12 walnuts

What to do:
Remove the walnut shells. Divide the walnuts in two. In a bowl, crush the cream cheese and mix with the Roquefort, cream and almonds. Spread this mixture with the blade of a knife on the slices of rye bread. Decorate with the walnuts.

Wine

Wine has had a long tradition in France and today vineyards are to be found all over France especially around Bordeaux, the Loire valley, Aquitaine, the Rhône valley, Burgundy, Champagne and Alsace. In 1985, France exported more than 50 million bottles of Champagne and 142 million bottles of Bordeaux wine.

Grape picking is an important activity in the autumn. Extra hands are always needed for the picking, and students often take this opportunity to make extra pocket-money. The grapes, once picked, are taken to the *chais* (wine houses) where those to be made into white wine are pressed immediately while those to be made into red wine are crushed and allowed to start fermenting before going into the *pressoirs* (wine presses).

With most areas of France producing their own wine, qualities and varieties differ a great deal.

Extra hands are always needed for grape picking. In this picture grape pickers enjoy lunch provided by the vineyard's owners.

Allowing the grapes to ferment at this stage gives time for the color to pass from the skins to the wine.

Certain wines go better with certain types of food. With fish, for example, a white wine would be chosen. Red wine is preferred with meat, and for dessert, a sweet wine, Champagne or other *mousseux* (sparkling wine) is a "must."

The vineyards around Bordeaux produce some of the best wines in the world. *Claret* is the name given by the British to a red Bordeaux wine. The greatest *crus* (wines of a good vintage) are from Médoc such as *Château-Lafite* and *Château Margaux* (red wines). The sweet, white *Sauternes*, also from this area, should be served very cool and is delicious with *foie gras*, fish and *Roquefort* cheese. In the Dordogne Valley two of the best wines to be found are the red *Saint-Emilion* and *Pomerol*.

A vineyard in Burgundy.

The Burgundy wines, including red *Nuits-Saint-Georges* and the white *Meursault* and *Chablis*, are almost as renowned as the Bordeaux wines. *Beaujolais* is a very popular red wine, and the *Beaujolais Nouveau* (the newest and youngest wine) is best drunk between November 15 and February 15.

The white wine, *Muscadet* from the Loire Valley, and the red wine *Châteauneuf-du-Pape* from the Rhône Valley, are also notable.

Alsace produces mostly white wines, such as *Gewürztraminer*, *Riesling* and *Sylvaner*. Corsica produces excellent wines (the white or rosé *Patrimonio*) and liqueurs such as *cédratine*.

There are important wine auctions and those in Beaune (in the Côte d'Or department) break records: a *Château-Lafite* (Bordeaux wine) bottled in 1806 was sold for thousands of dollars.

Many recipes include wine, the well-known *coq au vin* is one example. The French also drink beer, cider (especially in Normandy and Brittany) and mineral water. France is very rich in mineral waters with its springs of *Evian* (from Savoie), *Contrexeville*, *Vittel* (in the Vosges) and *Vichy* (from Auvergne).

Perhaps best known of all wines is Champagne. A seventeenth-century monk called Dom Pérignon was responsible for most of the development of this sparkling white wine.

Champagne is stored in cellars like these in special strengthened bottles.

Champagne is blended after fermentation in vats and then, unlike other wines, is sealed into strong bottles with a little yeast and sugar for a second fermentation. The resulting gas cannot escape and is dissolved into the wine to produce the bubbles. By law, Champagne is aged for at least three years before sale, although vintage Champagnes are matured for very much longer. Today, one-third of the Champagne produced is exported. In 1986, 16 million bottles were sent to Great Britain, which is the largest importing country.

Charente produces *cognac*, which is considered to be the best "pure" brandy in the world. Its origin dates back to the sixteenth century. After a double distillation in stills, *cognac* is put in big oak casks where it will age for at least three years. The older the brandy, the better it is.

Regional specialties

Brittany, Maine, Anjou and Touraine

Brittany is the most westerly part of France. All around the coast, a rich variety of fish are caught, from shellfish such as lobsters, crabs and clams, to mackerel, cod and sole. The area has its own fish stew called *cotriade*. Perhaps the most famous seafood of this region is the Belon oyster, raised in the oyster beds in the Gulf of Morbihan. Mussels are also farmed in this region and are harvested in special flat-bottomed boats at low tide.

Away from the coast there are

An oyster farm in the department of Morbihan. The woman in the picture is preparing slates for the oysters to cling to.

Artichokes, seen growing here, are produced in Brittany along with cauliflowers, onions and potatoes.

large market gardens growing artichokes, cauliflowers, onions (especially in Roscoff), strawberries and potatoes. Brittany also has a lot of dairy farms producing basic products such as milk, cream and butter. Pigs are also raised in the region and much of the pork meat is made into *andouilles* (chitterling sausages).

In the past, buckwheat was the only cereal cultivated in the Armorica, the upland area which forms the central part of Brittany. The population ate *crêpes* (pancakes) made of buckwheat flour instead of bread. Today the *crêpe* is still a national dish, and is sold at stands in the streets or eaten at *crêperies*, where they may be filled with egg and/or ham, or filled with chocolate, honey, jam or vanilla ice cream. They are often accompanied by the local cider.

The pastries from Brittany are also famous and the *farz* is a traditional Breton cake which varies slightly according to the town.

The *charcuteries* (delicatessens) in **Maine**, the region around Le Mans, Tours and Blois, sell *rillettes de porc*, which is shredded pork cooked with fat in a big pot and eaten cold on bread.

Anjou and **Touraine** are crossed by the Loire River which supplies salmon, pike and trout. The area is famous for its fish dishes. *Brochet au beurre blanc*, for instance, is pike cooked in water and vinegar and then served with a white sauce made with butter, shallots, vinegar and seasoning.

Normandy

The climate of **Normandy** favors dairy farming. The dairy industry is very important in this region which produces butter, cream, and several varieties of cheese. The butter of Isigny near Bayeux is said to be the best, and cream is used a lot in Norman cooking. *Moules à la crème*, for example, are mussels cooked in cream, *sole normande* is fillet of sole, caught off the Norman coast, simmered in water or white wine with mussels and shrimps and covered with thick cream.

In the spring the Norman countryside is full of apple blossoms. The apples grown in this region are turned into sweet or dry cider, as well as a strong spirit known as *Calvados*. This brandy is matured in casks for up to ten years and is traditionally drunk between courses to help digest your food.

Normandy is well known for its apples, which are made into cider and calvados. *Cider presses like the one in the picture have now mostly been replaced by mechanized presses.*

This pause in the meal to drink *Calvados* is called *trou normand* literally meaning "Norman hole."

Towns in Normandy have their own specialties; for example, Caen is famous for its *tripes à la mode de Caen*. This is a mixture of braised tripe which can be bought in ready-to-eat jars or cans.

Rouen also has a specialty. *Canard à la rouennaise* is lightly roasted duck, served with a rich blood sauce.

Picardy, Artois, Flanders, Ardennes and Champagne

These industrial regions in northern France are well known for potatoes, hops, wheat, sugar beets

and chicory. Potatoes are an important part of the diet in this area, as in neighboring Belgium, and are cooked in a variety of ways (see recipe).

Off the coasts of Dunkirk, Calais and Boulogne, fish such as herring and mackerel are caught and are served as a *matelote*, in which mixed fish are stewed together with onions and wine.

In the forest area of the Ardennes, which is near to both Belgium and Luxembourg, the specialty is smoked ham. Thrushes and wild boar are hunted in this area, and the game is turned into pâtés and roasts.

South of the Ardennes, Champagne is known more for its sparkling Champagne wine than for its cuisine. Champagne is not used widely in cooking although sometimes trout or salmon are served in a Champagne sauce.

Frogs' legs are popular in this region and are often used instead of meat in a *pot-au-feu*.

Gratin de pomme de terre (potato gratin)

You will need:
6 large potatoes
1 tablespoon butter, plus extra
   butter to put on top
2 pinches salt
2 cups milk
2 tablespoons grated cheese

What to do:
Peel and slice the potatoes. Heat the oven. Grease an ovenproof dish with the butter. Lay the potatoes on the bottom. Add the salt, milk and grated cheese. Put dots of butter on the top. Bake for 45 minutes in a 370° oven.
Safety note: Be careful when slicing the potatoes with the knife! Ask an adult to heat the oven and remove the dish when cooked.

Alsace, Lorraine and Franche-Comté

Alsace shares the Rhine as a border with Germany. Its vineyards produce mostly white wines such as *Riesling, Sylvaner* and *Gewürztraminer*. In the Vosges forests *framboises* (raspberries) and *myrtilles* (similar to blueberries) grow, as well as cherries which are made into kirsch (a brandy).

The *Kougelhof* is the traditional cake of this area. Sometimes baked

27

cramming apparatus is placed in the bill of the goose three times a day for a month. The liver of the goose swells so a goose of 10 kg (22 lbs) can have a liver weighing up to 1 kg (2.2 lb). *Foie gras* is very expensive and is considered to be a delicacy all over the world.

Lorraine uses a lot of pastry in its cooking. *Bouchée à la reine* is a pastry case filled with a mixture of chicken and mushrooms in a cream sauce. But perhaps the best known of Lorraine's pastry specialties is the *quiche*, a custard with pieces of ham covered with cream and egg yolks and baked in a pie shell (see recipe).

with raisins, it has a covering of almonds. The Alsatian tart, another specialty, is pastry filled with sliced apple, covered with a mixture of cream, egg yolks and kirsch and is then baked.

Alsace is influenced by neighboring Germany in much of its food and drink. Beer often accompanies meals, rather than the usual wine, and *choucroute garnie* is a great specialty. This is *sauerkraut* (fermented cabbage) which is topped with smoked pork, ham and sausages.

Alsace is also an important area for raising geese and making *foie gras*. Strasbourg especially has an excellent *pâté de foie gras* (goose liver pâté). Many people, however, think that the method used to obtain *foie gras* is very cruel. When the goose is four or five months old it is given, by force, enormous quantities of ground corn. A

A specialty of this region is choucroute garnie, *seen at the front of this picture.*

The **Franche-Comté**, south of Alsace and near Switzerland, is a region of mountains and forests, rich in mushrooms like *cèpes, morels* and *chanterelles*. In the streams crayfish can be found and are cooked first in white wine and then shelled and cooked again in cream.

Quiche Lorraine

You will need:
1 medium round quiche or pie pan
1 cup flour
3 tablespoons butter
3 tablespoons cold water
3 pinches salt
6 slices bacon
2 eggs
2 pinches salt
¾ cup cream
4 tablespoons of grated Gruyère or
   Swiss cheese

What to do:
(1) Place the flour, butter and salt in a bowl. Crumble fine with fingertips. Add the water, a little at a time, mixing to a dough. Place the dough on a floured surface and roll it out flat. (2) Line the bottom and sides of the greased quiche pan with the pastry and prick with a fork. Bake in a 375° oven for five minutes.

Cut the bacon into one-inch pieces, fry it and drain on paper towels. In a bowl, mix the eggs, salt, cream and grated cheese with a fork. Remove the pastry shell from the oven. (3) Lay the bacon in the pastry shell. Pour on the egg mixture. (4) Bake in a 375° oven for 30 minutes or until the filling is golden brown. Serve hot or cold with a salad.

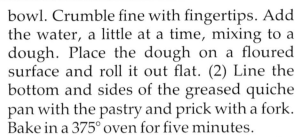

Burgundy and Berry

Below *The internationally known* boeuf Bourguignon *from Burgundy is cooked in wine from the region.*

The famous **Burgundy** wines are often used in cooking in what are called *meurettes*. The *meurette* of Burgundy consists of either meat or fish cooked in red wine with herbs and spices. This sauce is then thickened with a *beurre manie* (butter and flour).

Burgundy is particularly well known for its snails, which are popular throughout France. Burgundy snails are fatter and juicier than the snails to be found in the rest of France and are usually fried or stewed and served with garlic butter. *Boeuf bourguignon*, another popular dish from this region, is a rich beef stew made with wine and carrots.

Dijon, the capital of Burgundy, is

famous for its mustard, and also prides itself on its *pain d'épices* (spiced honey cakes).

Berry is an area of flat green countryside, west of Burgundy. The *Berrichons* (the people from this region) like hearty soups with cabbage, pumpkin, turnip, beans and potatoes. The best known specialties are *quenelles au jambon* (ham dumplings) and larks preserved in fat.

Savoie and Dauphiné

Savoie and **Dauphiné** are in the east of France, sharing borders along the Alps with Switzerland and Italy. The streams and lakes in the mountains are teeming with carp, trout, eel, pike and crayfish. Fish in this area is either fried, with cream, like *truites à la crème* (trout in cream), or cooked *au gratin*. In *gratin de queues d'écrevisse* (crayfish tail *gratin*), the crayfish are cooked in a thick cream of local cheese and butter and then cooked *au gratin*.

The cattle that graze in the Alps are of top quality, and their milk is used to make cheeses which may be used in *fondue* (the *fondue savoyarde* is a dish of melted *Beaufort* cheese) or in dishes cooked *au gratin*. The *gratin savoyard* (from Savoie) is different from the *gratin dauphinois* (from Dauphiné): both are made with sliced potatoes but the *gratin savoyard* is covered with grated *Beaufort* and stock, whereas the *gratin dauphinois* is covered with beaten eggs, cream and milk.

Tournedos dauphinois are thick boneless steaks served on a sauce of *cèpes* (mushrooms) and cream covered with a brown sauce made of local truffles.

Provence, Corsica and Languedoc Roussillon

Provence, in the southeast of France, is a Mediterranean province with a warm climate for most of the year. Provence stretches along the coast from the Rhône delta to the Italian border, and, inland, it takes in the southern part of the Alps and the fertile plains of the Rhône valley.

The coastline provides a lot of seafood. A famous dish is *bouillabaisse* (fish soup), which is made with Mediterranean fish such as *Saint-Pierre*, (John Dory), *vive*

The coastline of Provence provides a variety of seafood, much of which is used in the famous fish soup, bouillabaisse.

(weever fish), *rascasse* and sometimes *langoustes* (crayfish). These fish are cut into big chunks and cooked with olive oil, garlic, saffron and tomato.

Olive oil and garlic are often used in Provençal cooking, for example *aïoli* is a kind of mayonnaise made with garlic, bread crumbs soaked in milk and egg yolks. All this mixture is crushed and olive oil is poured on it. This sauce, to which pepper is added, is served with fish or boiled vegetables.

In the orchards around Avignon and Carpentras, peaches, pears, apricots, lemons and oranges grow, and the nearby town of Cavaillon is especially well known for its sweet

Ratatouille

You will need:
4 large peeled tomatoes
½ green pepper, sliced
1 zucchini, sliced
4 eggplant, sliced
2 cloves garlic, chopped
½ onion sliced
1 teaspoon salt
½ cup olive oil

What to do:
Cut each tomato into four pieces. Pour the olive oil into a saucepan or frying pan with a lid and heat. When hot, add the onion. Cook gently for 5 minutes. Then add tomatoes, pepper, eggplant, zucchini, garlic and salt. Put the lid on and cook for one hour. Delicious with rice.

Safety note: Wash the vegetables. Ask an adult to slice the vegetables and be careful of the hot oil.

melons. Vegetables from this region are used to make *ratatouille*, which can be served either hot or cold (see recipe).

Corsica is a mountainous French island in the Mediterranean Sea, 160 km (100 mi) from France and 80 km (50 mi) from Italy. Its food,

Corsican markets are always full of colour as you can see in the picture below of a confectionery stall.

however, is neither French nor Italian. The sea, of course, provides many fish and Corsica has its own *bouillabaisse* known as *u'ziminu*. Goats, sheep and ewes are raised in the mountains and the milk from the ewes produces the *broccio* cheese. A specialty is *pébronata* composed of braised kid (young goat) with peppers and white wine.

Languedoc-Roussillon is a sunny region lying along the Mediterranean coast between the Spanish border and the Camargue, the marshy rice-growing region of the Rhône delta, and inland it reaches as far as the southern part of the Massif Central.

Languedoc has a very rich variety of food: the *pot-au-feu* of Carcassonne is made of boiled beef and vegetables such as carrots, leeks and turnips plus mutton, bacon, stuffed cabbage and beans. Nîmes is famous for its *brandade de morue*, cod pounded with garlic,

Below One of France's best known cheeses, Roquefort, comes from Languedoc-Roussillon and is made from ewe's milk.

warm olive oil, cream and hot milk.

Toulouse, Carcassonne and Castelnaudary are very proud of their *cassoulet*, a garlic-flavored dish made of beans, lard, ham, pork-rind, herbs, and preserved goose.

The area is also the home of *Roquefort* cheese, made with the milk of ewes and matured in the natural caves of Roquefort-sur-Soulzon.

Roussillon, which neighbors Spain, is a big producer of fruit, such as peaches, pears, apricots, and nectarines and wines such as the *Corbières*, a table wine.

The Basque country, Béarn, Guyenne and Gascony

This southwestern region of France has many seafood specialties. The Atlantic Ocean in the west provides sardines, squid, tuna fish and oysters. The sardines are grilled in the restaurants in the ports of Biarritz and Saint-Jean-de-Luz on the Basque coastline. Squid, called *chipirons* by the Basque people, are served in a spicy tomato sauce, and the *thon Basquaise* is tuna fish cooked with peppers, tomatoes, eggplant and garlic (see recipe). Oysters are farmed in the Bay of Arcachon, to the south of Bordeaux.

Thon Basquaise (tuna Basquaise)

You will need:
1¼ lb fresh tuna fish
green pepper
4 peeled tomatoes
1 eggplant
1 large onion, chopped
1 clove garlic
thyme
flour
olive oil

What to do:
(1) Roll the tuna in the flour. Pour olive oil into a pan, heat it and brown the fish. Remove from pan. Cut the tomatoes into pieces and cook them in the oil. (2) Dice the eggplant and add to the tomatoes with onion and garlic. (3) When the vegetables are soft, add thyme, salt, pepper and the tuna. Let it simmer gently for 20 minutes. (4) Serve with rice.

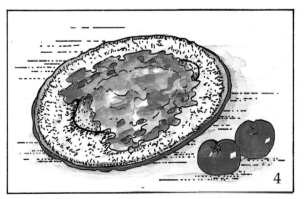

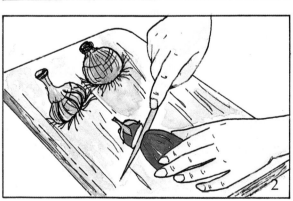

Above *A shop in Pau, the capital of Béarn, with Bayonne hams hanging from the ceiling.*

The hilly **Basque country** between the Pyrenees and the ocean has its own fish soup called *ttoro. Piperade* is an egg dish from this region made with Bayonne ham, tomatoes and pimentos (types of peppers that are very hot). It also has *poulet basquaise*, chicken cooked with tomatoes, and *touron*, confectionery made with ground almonds, eggs and sugar.

Bayonne, situated 30 km (21 mi) from Spain, is well known for its salt-cured hams and delicious chocolate. Moving eastward toward **Béarn** the popular dish is *garbure*, a soup made with pork and vegetables. Henry IV, who was born in Pau, the capital of Béarn, in 1553, had wanted to see chicken in every peasant's pot on Sundays.

For this reason, the *poule au port*, stuffed boiled chicken and vegetables, is popular to this day in the region.

In **Gascony**, especially in the Landes, a vast region of moors and pine trees, and in Périgord, the region around Périgueux in **Guyenne**, geese can be seen in the farmyards, and even crossing the roads!

This is another area where the geese are force-fed to give the huge livers for *pâté de foie gras* (see page 28), and goosefat is used, instead of

Small children selling cèpes *in the woods near Bordeaux.*

butter or oil, in much of the local cooking.

South of Agen, the region of Armagnac has given its name to a very strong brandy. The plum trees in the region of Agen produce plums which are then dried. These are the famous *pruneaux d'Agen*, which are often sold as confectionery in big jars full of Armagnac brandy.

In addition to its fine wines, Bordelais (Bordeaux region) is famous for its good food. The *entrecôte bordelaise*, for instance, is a rib of beef with a sauce made of cooked red wine, minced shallots and melted butter. *Cèpes à la bordelaise* are wild mushrooms cooked in olive oil, with chopped shallot, garlic and parsley. *Cèpes* grow in the woods in autumn and those around Bordeaux are big, dark-brown and are particularly well known.

Périgord is the homeland of truffles, *foie gras* and *confits*. The truffle is a fungus growing underground, and pigs or trained dogs help to sniff out the truffles. They are used for flavoring savory dishes, but today they are rare and extremely costly. *Confits* are pieces of goose or duck, left in salt for twenty-four hours, cooked and then preserved in fat, in earthenware pots.

Sows are trained to find the rare and expensive truffles in Périgord.

Charente, Poitou and Limousin

Charente is south of Brittany and its most important port is La Rochelle. Tuna fish, swordfish, sardines and elver (young eels) are caught here. They are most commonly cooked in white wine with shallots and butter. Such dishes are known as *chaudrée*.

Rich pastures inland in the region

Clafouti Limousin

You will need:
8 eggs
4 cups milk
4 tablespoons sugar
1½ lb cherries (or strawberries or raspberries)
butter

What to do:
(1) Whisk the eggs and sugar together and then whisk in the milk. Remove the stems from the cherries and wash them. Grease an ovenproof dish with some of the butter. (2) Put the cherries in the dish then pour on the mixture of eggs and sugared milk. (3) Fill a large, shallow dish or roasting pan with water and place the dish with the mixture in it. Dot the top of the pudding with flakes of butter. (4) Bake in a preheated 400° oven for 30 minutes, or until custard is firm, and serve.

Safety note: Ask an adult to take the dish out of the oven as it will be very hot.

neighboring **Limousin**. Limousin is the home of *marrons* (chestnuts) which are either used to make *purée limousine* with mashed cabbage, or are candied to make *marrons glacés*, which are exported around the world. In summer the dessert of this region is *clafouti*, a soft creamy cake with lots of cherries (see recipe).

Auvergne and Lyonnais

of Charente-Poitou are grazing land for cattle. The butter made in this region is particularly good, and the creamy cheese, *chabichou*, is made in **Poitou** (the region around Poitiers) from goats' milk.

Cognac, a town in Charente is the home of *cognac* brandy, which is matured in oak casks from

The old harbor, La Rochelle, where tuna, swordfish, sardines and elver are caught.

The **Auvergne** is in the heart of the Massif Central, a large and very old range of extinct volcanic mountains in the center of France. The land is relatively poor and hard to cultivate so the population lives on a simple cuisine based on cabbage, potatoes, lentils and pork. *Potée auvergnate*, which consists of sausages, salted pork (*petit salé*), potatoes and onions is typical of this region. The cows grazing in Auvergne's high pastures produce milk that is used to make cheeses such as *Cantal* and *Bleu d'Auvergne*, which is a salty blue cheese.

Lyonnais (around Lyons) is a small but prosperous area in the Rhône region. The people of Lyons regard their city as the capital of French gastronomy. The region certainly benefits from the products of its neighbors. To the north there is Burgundy with its wines and *charolais* beef, and there are corn-fed chickens from Bresse. To the south there is the fertile Rhône Valley with its fruit and vegetables. To the west is Auvergne and to the east Savoie and Switzerland.

A charcuterie *stand in Lyons. The city is particularly well known for its* saucissons.

In the eighteenth century the *charcuterie* (cold cuts) of Lyons were known throughout all Europe, especially the *saucisson* (dried sausage) made with Champagne and truffles. The great regional dish is the *poulet demi-deuil* ("chicken in half-mourning"): before the chicken is poached, slices of black truffle are slid under the skin giving the chicken a blackish appearance. Many of the best French cooks are either from Lyons, or from nearby. The great chef Paul Bocuse is the descendant of a family that started cooking in 1765 in a restaurant at Collonges-au-Mont-d'Or, very near Lyons, and the famous brothers Pierre and Michel Troisgros have a restaurant in Roanne, 60 km (38 mi) west of Lyons.

Paris, Île-de-France and Orléanais

The region around Paris is called the **Île-de-France**. All the best ingredients from the provinces of France are brought here to feed the population of the capital. For this reason, Paris and its neighborhood has gradually become the center of French gastronomy.

Paris is well known for its *baguette*, (long thin bread), which is sold everywhere in France. Its pastry cooks are real artists, preparing *croissants*, *brioches*, *éclairs* filled with chocolate or coffee cream and *mille-feuilles*, made from fragile flaky pastry filled with vanilla or coffee cream.

Île-de-France produces its own soft cheeses, such as *Coulommiers* and *Brie*, both of which are made from cows' milk. In caves around Paris little white mushrooms

are cultivated which are an important ingredient in many of the dishes of the region.

South and southwest of Paris is the Beauce area, the "granary" of France with vast wheatfields surrounding the city of Chartres.

Orléanais (the area surrounding Orléans) produces some of the world's finest vinegars which, unlike most other vinegars, are produced in two stages, rather than the usual one, and are kept in casks for three to four months before bottling. This region is also the major food-canning area of France.

The baguette, *a specialty of Paris, is now sold all over France.*

41

Festive food

The French enjoy celebrating all year round, and weddings, baptisms and first communions are always occasions for big meals with lots of guests. Such meals usually finish with the magnificent *pièce montée* (set-piece), which is a huge cake made by placing lots of cream-filled *profiteroles* (round pastries) on top of each other to make a pyramid, sometimes more than three feet high. Caramel is then poured over it all and a decoration

The man on the left of this picture is serving the pièce montée *at a wedding.*

put on the very top – a cradle for a baptism or a married couple for a wedding. After the religious service, *dragées* (sugared almonds) are thrown to the children.

Christmas and New Year's Day are big feasts for the whole family and friends. The tradition is to celebrate Christmas at home and to go out to a restaurant to see the New Year in. On these occasions, at about midnight, an elaborate meal is served with a variety of courses. The menu may include *pâté de foie gras*, *galantine*, *boudin* (blood sausage) or white *boudin* (with the

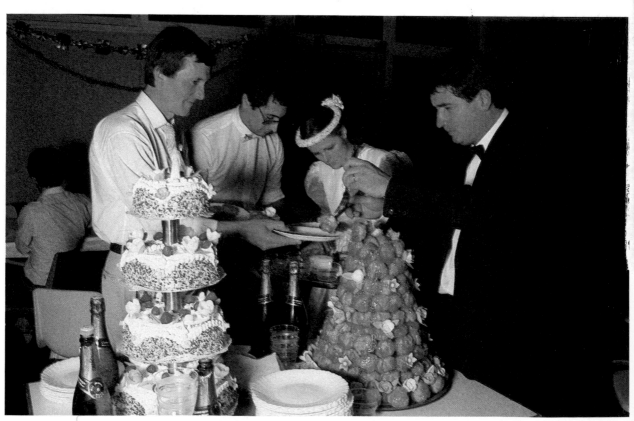

42

First communions are important occasions and a time to celebrate with special food.

addition of milk), roast turkey with chestnuts, game, fish, oysters, lobsters, crayfish, caviar, smoked salmon, truffles from Périgord and of course the *bûche de Noel*, a long, log-shaped cake filled with vanilla, chocolate or coffee cream. The best wines and Champagnes are always served to accompany these meals.

On Epiphany Day (January 6) the custom is to eat the *gâteau des rois* (king's cake). It is traditional for the youngest member in the family to cut the cake and portion it out. The one who finds the *fève* (favor) in his or her slice will be king for the day and gets to wear a crown of golden paper. The king is obliged to offer Champagne, wine, cider or another cake. (In the past, the *fève* was a bean, but today it has been replaced by a plastic object in the shape of a star, or a moon.)

Chandeleur (Candlemas) falls on February 2 and celebrates the presentation of Jesus at the Temple in Jerusalem. It is the time for making pancakes, waffles, or fritters (in the south).

At Easter, children hunt for chocolate eggs that have been hidden by their parents in the house or garden. The stores at this time are full of eggs, chickens, bells and fish all made of chocolate. The Easter meal is traditionally lamb with small green kidney beans.

French food abroad

France has a long tradition of great chefs, and wherever they have gone in the world, the art of French cookery has gone with them. Antoine Carême, who was born in 1784 and was a famous chef of his time, was employed by the Regent (later George IV) of England. Carême was taken to the Regent's palace, the Royal Pavilion in Brighton, England, to act as chef. He was particularly well known for his *pièces montées* (see page 42).

Another famous French chef was Georges-Auguste Escoffier who was chef at the Savoy Hotel in London from 1890 to 1899. Artists, writers and other fortunate people would visit the places where Escoffier was cooking, and, to please his customers, he named dishes after them. *Pêche Melba*, for example, was named after the famous singer Nellie Melba.

Today, in capital cities all over the world there are French restaurants that serve the finest French food, cooked by the finest French chefs. Hotels too, especially the larger and more expensive ones, employ French chefs who are considered the best in the world.

The great cooks of today, such as Paul Bocuse, Michel Guerard and the Troisgros brothers, not only run their own restaurants but also travel abroad to give lectures and make television programs about French cooking.

With this growing interest in French food and cooking, the demand for French exports abroad has also grown. France exports bread, wine, cheese and many specialties such as *foie gras*. Bakers have settled abroad, especially in the United States, and set up businesses making French bread and *croissants*. The baker Poilâne sells bread in Tokyo, Berlin, Riyadh. Some Chinese and Japanese people have even gone to Paris to learn Poilâne's baking methods.

Paul Bocuse is one of the world's greatest chefs.

Glossary

Apéritif An alcoholic drink drunk before a meal to whet the appetite.

Au Gratin Topped with bread-crumbs and sometimes cheese, and browned in the oven.

Brandy An alcoholic liquor distilled from the fermented juice of grapes or other fruits and used as an after-dinner drink.

Bourgeoisie The bourgeois, or middle classes.

Brioches Soft rolls or loaves made from a very light yeast mixture sometimes mixed with currants.

Caviar The salted roe (eggs) of sturgeon (a large fish).

Chitterlings The intestines of a pig or other animal, prepared as a dish.

Crayfish A freshwater shellfish that looks like a small lobster.

Delicatessen Delicacies such as especially prepared meat and cheeses or a store selling such foods.

Earthenware Pottery made of baked clay.

EEC The European Economic Community or Common Market. A group of European countries formed on January 1, 1958, for the purpose of making special arrangements for buying and selling each others' products, making laws and deciding other important matters that affect each member country.

Fermentation A slow change in a substance brought about by adding something, such as yeast, that produces chemical changes.

Fertile Providing large crops. Fertile soil is rich so crops grow well.

Galantine A cold dish of meat or poultry that is boned, cooked and stuffed, then pressed into a meat shape and glazed with jelly.

Gourmet An expert and critical judge of food and drink.

Hors d'oeuvre An additional dish served as an appetizer, usually before the main course.

Quenelles Finely sieved mixture of cooked meat or fish shaped into various forms and cooked in stock or fried.

Saffron A yellow seasoning used for flavoring or coloring food.

Shallots A kind of small onion.

Table wine A wine considered suitable for drinking with a meal.

Tripe Parts of the stomach of sheep and cattle that are used as food.

French words and phrases

Food

Le beurre	Butter
Le boeuf	Beef
Le café	Coffee
Le fromage	Cheese
Un gâteau	A cake
La glace	Ice cream
Le lait	Milk
Les legumes	Vegetables
Le pain	Bread
Le poisson	Fish
Le poulet	Chicken
La salade	Salad
Le thé	Tea
Une tomate	A tomato
Le veau	Veal
Le vin	Wine

At the restaurant

Garçon!	Waiter!
La serveuse	The waitress
J'ai faim	I'm hungry
J'ai soif	I'm thirsty
S'il vous plait	Please
Merci	Thank you

Puis je voir la carte?
May I see the menu?
Je voudrais du thon Basquaise
I would like tuna Basquaise
Qu'est-ce que vous avez comme desserts?
What desserts do you have?
L'addition, s'il vous plait
The bill, please.

Typical menu

Hors d'oeuvres
Crudités
ou
Pâté de maison

Les poissons
Thon Basquaise
ou
Truites à la crème

Les Viandes
Sauté de veau Marengo
ou
Entrecôte bordelaise

Fromages

Les Desserts
Sorbet
ou
Clafouti limousin

Café

Further reading

Betty Crocker's Cookbook for Boy's and Girls. Western Publishers, 1984.

Cooking the French Way by Lynne Villios. Lerner Publications, 1982.

Cooking of Provincial France by M.F. Fisher. Silver, 1968.

The Fannie Farmer Junior Cookbook by Wilma L. Perkins. Little, 1957.

Follow the Sun: International Cookbook for Young People by Mary Deming and Joyce Haddard. Sun Scope, 1982.

French Regional Menus, A Time Life Book. Silver, 1984.

Growing Up in France by Sabra Holbrook. Atheneum, 1980.

The Land and People of France, rev.ed., by Lillian J. Bragdon. Harper & Row, 1972.

Take a Trip to France by Jonathan Rutland. Franklin Watts, 1981.

We Live in France by James Tomlins. Franklin Watts, 1984.

Index

Picture Acknowledgments

The publishers would like to thank the following for their permission to reproduce copyright pictures: Anthony Blake 12 (top), 14, 18 (left), 30, 40, 44 Cephas Picture Library 11, 13 (top), 18 (right), 21 (bottom), 22 (top), 24, 25, 42 Greg Evans Photo Library *cover*, 8 (bottom), 16 Denis Hughes-Gilbey 7, 9, 20, 28, 32, 34, 36, 37, 43 Hutchison Library 21 (top), 26 Mancini/Hughes-Gilbey 13 (bottom) Christine Osborne 4, 33 ZEFA 6, 8 (top), 10, 12 (bottom), 22 (bottom), 23, 39, 41. The map on page 5 is by David Noble. The regional specialities maps are by Malcolm Walker. All step-by-step illustrations are by Juliette Nicholson.